recycling & reusing

Paper

Ruth Thomson

Photography by Neil Thomson

A⁺

Smart Apple Media

First published in 2006 by Franklin Watts
338 Euston Road, London NW1 3BH

Franklin Watts Australia, Hachette Children's Books
Level 17/207 Kent Street, Sydney NSW 2000

Series editor: Rachel Cooke, Series design: Holly Mann, Art Director: Rachel Hamdi

Text copyright © Ruth Thomson 2006
Photographs copyright © Neil Thomson 2006

Additional photography
SCA Forest Products 8; Ecoscene/Sally Morgon 9tl; Aylesford Newsprint 9bl; Recycle now 9r, 21br, 24t; Warmcel 25b; Galloway Recycled Newspapers 25t; Hans Hansen (Hamburg, Germany) and Frank Gehry 27l.

Published in the United States by Smart Apple Media
2140 Howard Drive West, North Mankato, Minnesota 56003

Library of Congress Cataloging-in-Publication Data

Thomson, Ruth, 1949-
Paper / by Ruth Thomson.
p. cm. — (Recycling and reusing)
Includes index.
ISBN-13: 978-1-58340-940-4
1. Paper—Juvenile literature. I. Title.

TS1105.5.T66 2006
676'.142—dc22   2006000021

9 8 7 6 5 4 3 2 1

Contents

What is paper like?

Imagine how different life would be without paper.

There would be no books or newspapers, no writing paper, dollar bills, notebooks, or tissues. There would be no cardboard for packaging and protecting things. Paper is a very useful **material**.

Paper is thin, light, and flat. You can write, print, and draw on paper.

Paper is easy to cut or tear. You can cut it into any shape.

Paper is easy to join. You can join it with glue, staples, or tape.

Paper is flexible.
You can fold it.

An **origami** figure from Japan

You can roll it.

A pencil
holder
from India

You can weave it.

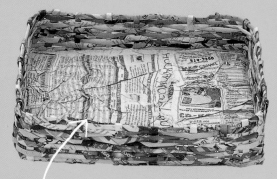

A basket from Brazil

Paper can be strong.
Cardboard is strong, thick, and stiff. It is made from several layers of paper pressed together.

Corrugated cardboard has a spongy, wavy layer inside. It is especially strong.

Corrugated
cardboard boxes

A cardboard box

Oops!
When most paper gets wet, it becomes soft and soggy and falls apart.

Making paper

Paper is made from long, thin threads, known as **fibers**, found in plants.

Plantations for paper

Most paper is made from **conifer trees**, such as pine and fir. This is because their wood has long, strong fibers.

Conifer trees are grown on **plantations** in cold places such as Scandinavia and Canada. Once they are **felled**, new trees are planted in their place.

LOOK AND SEE

Tear a piece of paper and look at its torn edge through a magnifying glass. Can you see hairy fibers sticking out?

Paper pulp

Logs are taken to a pulp mill. They are chopped into wood chips and mixed with chemicals. The mixture is heated until it becomes a mushy **pulp**. The pulp is cleaned and sometimes **bleached**, and is then ready for paper-making.

At the paper mill

The pulp is taken to a **paper mill**, where it is beaten with hot water into a smooth liquid. This is spread onto a long, moving wire **mesh**. As the mesh shakes, water drains out. The fibers tangle and form a soggy sheet.

The sheet is flattened between heavy **rollers**, which squeeze out more water. Heated rollers then dry the sheet. The fibers stick together to make paper.

Finally, heavy, iron rollers, called calenders, smooth and polish the paper before it is wound onto a huge reel.

9

YOUR TURN

Collect all kinds of paper— writing paper, paper towels, wax paper, tissue paper, toilet paper, paper bags, newspaper, wrapping paper, and magazines.

- *Compare the way they feel. Which is the softest? Which is the smoothest? Which is the best for writing on?*
- *See how easy they are to tear, crumple, or fold. Which is the strongest?*
- *Notice which paper is best at soaking up liquids.*

Reusing paper

A huge amount of paper is made just for things that are thrown away soon after they have been used.

People throw away food wrappers, newspapers, magazines, and used paper. They also **discard** paper cups and plates. In countries where paper is scarce or expensive, people reuse paper in all sorts of ways.

A cone to carry

In many places, food vendors sell snacks, such as nuts and seeds, wrapped in cones of discarded office paper or pages of old school books.

Paper bags

In India, some people make a living by gluing newspaper or magazine pages together to make paper bags.

A bendable basket

This origami basket was made from pages of a discarded magazine. Squares of paper were folded several times and tucked into one another.

Terrific toys

In parts of Africa and India, people make cheap toys from old newspaper. These are often sold at festivals.

Here are some ideas for saving paper. Can you think of any more?

- Write and print on both sides of every sheet.
- Cut up old greetings cards to make gift tags.
- Staple scrap paper together to make notepads.
- Reuse envelopes. Stick a label over the old address.
- Reuse wrapping paper.
- Donate old books to hospitals or charities.

This library in South Africa is stocked with books donated by other countries.

Rolling ahead

Paper becomes much stronger when it is rolled up.

Paper rolling

In Brazil, paper rolling is a popular way of reusing newspaper and magazine pages. People make both useful and decorative objects. The words and pictures on the paper create interesting patterns.

Making paper tubes

This girl has rolled sheets of paper, one at a time, around a stick. She glued down the loose end and removed the stick. Then she wove the tubes together.

Basket

Side by side

The tubes are also glued side by side to decorate things made of cardboard.

A jewelry box

Shelves

Rolled paper pieces

People in other countries use rolled paper in different ways.

Jewelry from South Africa

A letter rack from India

A braided hat from India

A container from Vietnam

13

Lots of layers

Sometimes, waste paper can be used to make useful bowls and dishes.

sardine can

labels

Paper bowls

In South Africa, a group of women earn money by making colorful paper bowls decorated with labels from fish cans.

1. They paste layers of scrap white paper over a plastic bowl. This makes a paper bowl shape.

3. They glue overlapping strips around the bowl, inside and out. Finally, they add a coat of **varnish**.

2. They cut fish can labels into dozens of thin strips.

A finished bowl

Make a paper dish or bowl of your own, either for yourself or to give away.

- Tear newspaper and colored scrap paper into small pieces, keeping the two piles separate.
- Cover a plastic or ceramic bowl with plastic wrap.
- Mix equal amounts of water and glue.

1. Paste several layers of paper over the bowl. Alternate the two kinds so you can see when you have finished each layer.

2. Allow your bowl to dry completely. Then remove it from the bowl or tray.

3. Paint the bowl in bright colors (above) or glue on overlapping paper scraps (below).

Molded masks

At some festivals in India, people wear paper masks made from old newspaper.

Making a mask

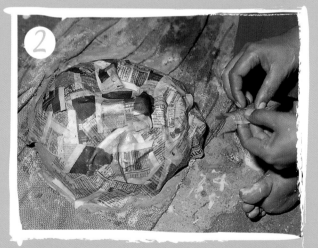

1. A mask-maker models a face in damp clay. This will be the shape of the mask.

2. He covers this with layers of newspaper pieces dipped in starch and water. The starch is like glue. It sticks the newspaper together.

3. The mask-maker allows the newspaper to dry. Then he carefully takes the mask off the clay face and paints it in bright colors.

Finally, he varnishes the mask to make it strong and waterproof.

Some masks are spectacular!

Pulped paper

Some white waste paper is made into paper pulp.

Making paper pulp

The paper is soaked in water for several days until it falls apart. Then people pound the pulp to make it smooth and creamy. They add starch to make it stronger.

Shaped by hand

In Bihar, in northeast India, women model paper pulp by hand. They often create animals, especially cows, to sell to tourists.

When the animals are dry, the women paint patterns and designs on them.

Play the game

Ludo is a game that was invented in India. This Ludo board, pieces, dice, and shaker are all made from paper pulp.

Made in a mold

Kashmiris from northern India make boxes and bowls from pulp. They press it around clay or wooden **molds**. When the pulp is dry, they cut the shape off the mold. Then they smooth and paint it.

They decorate the bowls with patterns and pictures of local trees, flowers, and animals. They add the final details in gold paint.

19

Recycling paper

All sorts of used paper can be recycled into new paper.

Waste not, want not

Waste paper is sorted at a paper mill before being beaten with water into a pulp. Whirling machines remove any printing ink, glue, staples, and other unwanted materials. The clean pulp is turned into new paper, cardboard, or **newsprint**.

Making recycled paper uses fewer chemicals, less water, and less **energy** than making new paper.

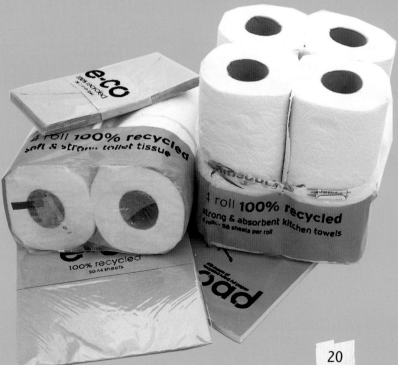

Recycled paper

High-quality white waste paper from offices and industry is often recycled into new writing or computer paper.

Lower-quality paper is made into toilet paper or paper towels.

Spot the signs

Whenever you buy recycled paper and recycling paper, you help the **environment**. Look for these signs on paper products.

IT'S A FACT

You CAN recycle:

✔ white office paper
✔ magazines
✔ newspapers
✔ junk mail
✔ catalogs
✔ cardboard

You CANNOT recycle:

✘ greasy pizza boxes
✘ egg cartons
✘ waxed cups and plates
✘ wax-coated cardboard

YOU CAN HELP

Save all your waste paper, newspapers, magazines, paper packaging, and cardboard for recycling.

Put them in a paper recycling bin or leave them out for a curbside collector.

Handmade paper

Some white waste paper is recycled into individual sheets of handmade paper.

Paper making

3. The paper is tipped onto a sheet of felt, which soaks up more water. Then it is stacked with other sheets in a press. The press squeezes out even more water.

1. Paper is shredded, then soaked and broken into pulp. The pulp is mixed with more water in a vat.

2. A mold and deckle are dipped into the pulp. When they are lifted up, water drains out, leaving a soggy sheet.

4. Finally, the sheets are separated and hung up to dry.

Pretty paper

Sometimes, cotton, flower petals, grasses, tea leaves, and even elephant dung (which contains plant fibers) are added to pulp to create textured paper.

paper with flower petals

bark-dyed paper

cotton paper

elephant dung paper

reed paper

Patterned paper

In South Africa, some handmade paper is dipped in brown dye made from tree bark.

People use bleach to paint on patterns. This whitens parts of the paper again.

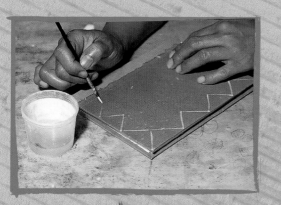

Notebook

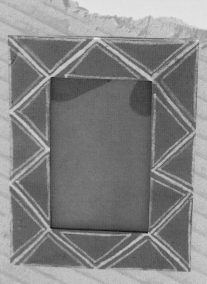

Picture frame

Napkin rings

New uses for old newspapers

Over a quarter of old newspapers are recycled to make newsprint.

The ink is washed off. Then the paper is turned back into pulp and mixed with new pulp for paper-making.

Molded pulp

Egg boxes and fruit trays are made from newspaper pulp, which is shaped in a mold. The pulp is dried in an oven and then removed from the mold.

LOOK AND SEE

Rip a sheet of newspaper and a piece of white paper from top to bottom. Notice how much easier the newspaper is to tear. This is because its fibers are much shorter.

24

Animal bedding

Shredded newspaper can be used as soft bedding for horses and cows.

It is warm, absorbent, and less dusty than straw. After use, it is mixed with water and spread on fields as a fertilizer.

IT'S A FACT

Newspaper cannot be recycled as many times as white paper. This is because its fibers are short and weaker.

As many as 4,000 trees are needed to make the paper for one day's edition of a newspaper in a big city.

Keeping homes warm

Finely ground newspaper can be sprayed between the inner and outer walls of new houses to keep in heat.

Cardboard constructions

Poor-quality paper and cardboard are usually recycled into corrugated cardboard.

Cardboard collectors

In Africa, Asia, and South America, **sanitation workers** earn a living by collecting discarded cardboard from shops and businesses. They sell it back to factories for recycling.

All sorts of boxes

In Egypt, small workshops cut, shape, and staple sheets of recycled cardboard into shoe boxes.

The boxes are covered with recycled paper labels.

A cardboard chair

Frank Gehry, a renowned architect, designed this chair made from recycled cardboard. He called it a "Wiggle chair."

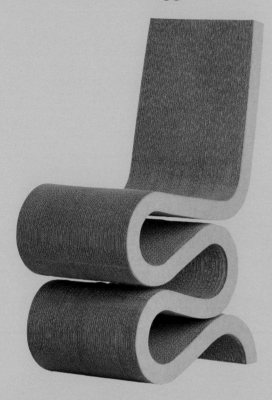

Disposable furniture

About 400,000 pieces of furniture were needed for the Olympic Games village in Sydney, Australia, in 2000. The organizers used cardboard chairs and tables. Wooden or metal ones would have been far bulkier to move and harder to sell. Once the Games were over, the furniture was recycled into newsprint.

Make a striking poster encouraging people to recycle all of their paper and cardboard.

RECYCLE
ALL
YOUR PAPER

Put it up in a place where people can see it as a useful reminder.

Glossary

bleached lightened or whitened with a chemical called bleach

conifer tree an evergreen tree that grows in cold climates and has thin, sharp, needle-like leaves and cones

discard throw away

energy the power that drives machines

environment the world around us— the land, sea, and air

fell to chop down a tree

fiber a thin strand that makes up plants, including trees

flexible able to bend without breaking

material a substance used to make something else

mesh crisscrossed wires with tiny holes between them

mold a hollowed-out shape; if paper pulp is put into a mold, or around it, it takes on the shape of the mold

mold and deckle handmade paper-making equipment; the mold is a frame with wire mesh stretched over it, and the deckle is a frame with edges that sit on top of the mold to hold the paper pulp in place

newsprint the type of paper used for printing newspapers

origami the Japanese art of folding paper into shapes

paper mill a factory where paper is made

papyrus a tall reed that grows by the Nile River in Egypt; papyrus is also the name given to the kind of paper made from the sliced pith of the papyrus stem

plantation a large area of land used for growing only one type of plant, such as conifer trees, tea, coffee, or bananas

pulp a mixture of soft, broken-down fibers and water

roller something in the shape of a cylinder that turns like a wheel

sanitation worker someone who collects and sorts garbage

varnish a clear material coated over another the surface of another one to protect it and make it shine

Guess what?

- It takes between six months and one year for paper to rot.
- Paper makes up more than 30 percent of all household garbage.
- In the United States, each person uses about 700 pounds (318 kg) of paper products every year.
- Newspapers contain an average of 50 percent recycled paper.

Useful Web sites

http://www.epa.gov/recyclecity/
See how Dumptown became Recycle City with fun games and interesting facts about recycling paper and other materials

http://kid-at-art.com/
Creative art projects to make with recycled materials and links to other art Web sites

http://www.olliesworld.com/planet/
A fun, interactive Web site that includes information and tips about reusing and recycling paper

http://www.planetpals.com/earthday.html
Projects and information about Earth Day, America Recycles Day, and other events that promote recycling

http://www.tappi.org/paperu
Includes facts about trees, the history of paper-making, recycling and the environment, as well as art and science projects

http://www.thomasrecycling.com/
kids.html
Tips, facts, and information about recycling

Index